Let's learn some interesting facts about **Russia!**

The official
name for Russia
is the Russian
Federation.

Russia shares borders with many countries—China, Ukraine, North Korea and Norway.

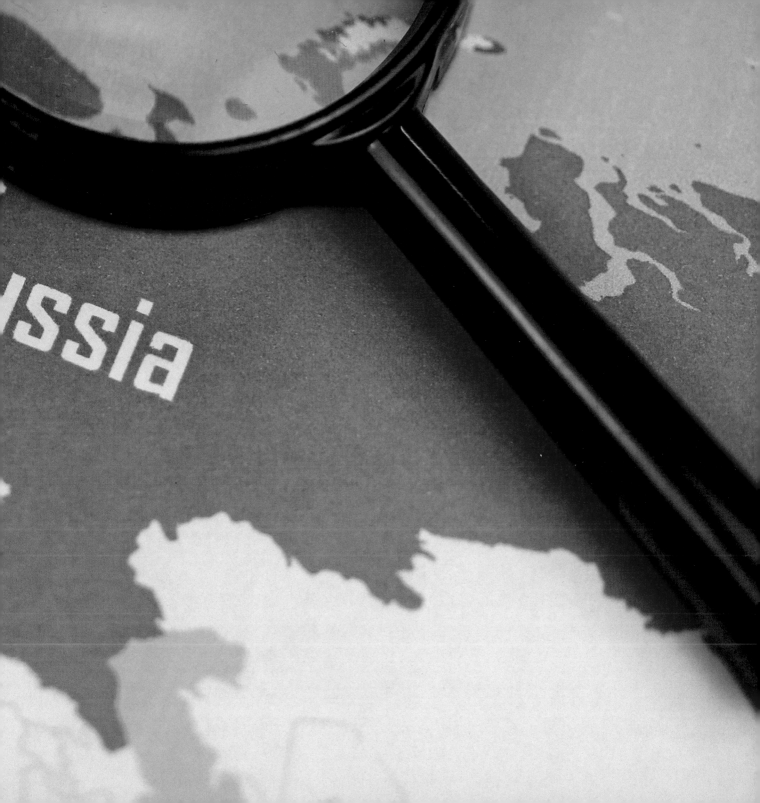

Russia was estimated to have a population of around 143 million.

Russia is the largest country in the world in terms of land area.

Russia has 9 time zones across the country.

The capital
and largest
city in Russia
is Moscow.

The currency used in Russia is the ruble.

Russia is rich of natural resources and is one of the world's largest producers of oil.

The Soviet Union (USSR) was a socialist state that occupied much of northern Asia and eastern Europe from 1922 until it was dissolved in 1991.

The official residence of the Russian president is the Kremlin in Moscow which means fortress.

Russia has over 40 national parks and 100 wildlife reserves.

Lake Baikal is the largest freshwater lake in the world. It reaches 1642 metres (5,387 feet) in depth and contains around 20% of the world's unfrozen fresh water.

Mount Elbrus is the highest mountain in Russia (and Europe), it reaches a height of 5642 metres (18,510 feet).

Volga River is the longest in Europe, with a length of around 3690 kilometres (2293 miles).

Russia has the world's largest area of forests.

Russia produces a large amount of renewable energy.

Basketball, ice hockey and football are popular sports in Russia.

Russia has a lot to offer and you should visit the country soon and explore!

42331800R00024

Made in the USA
San Bernardino, CA
01 December 2016